D1519111

LIVING FOSSILS

Sponges

Ryan Nagelhout

PowerKiDS press.

New York

Published in 2015 by The Rosen Publishing Group, Inc.
29 East 21st Street, New York, NY 10010

First Edition

Editor: Sarah Machajewski
Book Design: Mickey Harmon

Photo Credits: Cover, pp. 1–24 (border); cover (logo texture), pp. 1–3, 4, 6, 10, 12, 14, 16, 20, 22–24 (background texture); cover (tube sponge), pp. 18–19 (ocean background) Ocean Image Photography/Shutterstock.com; cover (coral reef), p. 13 Rich Carey/Shutterstock.com; p. 5 LauraD/Shutterstock.com; p. 7 (sponge) Jad Davenport/National Geographic/Getty Images; p. 7 (pores) Cavan Images/The Image Bank/Getty Images; pp. 8–9 DJ Mattaar/Shutterstock.com; p. 15 Reinhard Dirscherl/Shutterstock.com; p. 17 Jeff Rotman/Photolibrary/Getty Images; p. 18 (basket of sponges) Fox Photos/Hulton Archive/Getty Images; p. 19 (dried sponges) Walter Bibikow/AWL Images/Getty Images; p. 21 j loveland/Shutterstock.com; p. 22 (sponge) Amanda Nicholls/Shutterstock.com.

Library of Congress Cataloging-in-Publication Data

Nagelhout, Ryan, author.
 Sponges / Ryan Nagelhout.
     pages cm. — (Living fossils)
 Includes index.
 ISBN 978-1-4777-5842-7 (pbk.)
 ISBN 978-1-4777-5840-3 (6 pack)
 ISBN 978-1-4777-5844-1 (library binding)
 1. Sponges—Juvenile literature. 2. Living fossils—Juvenile literature. I. Title.
 QL371.6.N34 2015
 593.4—dc23
                              2014028314

Manufactured in the United States of America

CPSIA Compliance Information: Batch #CW15PK: For Further Information contact Rosen Publishing, New York, New York at 1-800-237-9932

Contents

Super Sponges

Have you ever used a sponge when you take a bath? It was likely man-made. Did you know there's another kind of sponge? It's an animal that has been around for hundreds of millions of years. Thousands of these ancient animals live in waters all over the world.

Sponges were among the first animals on Earth. One of the earliest-known animals was a tiny sponge fossil, or hardened remains, that was found in a 760-million-year-old rock in Africa. The animal was only the size of a grain of sand, but sponges such as that changed the planet forever.

FOSSIL FACTS

Some scientists think sponges put **oxygen** into Earth's waters 700 million years ago. This made it possible for other life-forms to grow.

Sponges like the ones pictured here have had a great effect on Earth's waters.

Holey Moly!

Sponges are part of a group of animals called Porifera, which means "pore bearers." A pore is a hole that lets things pass through it. A sponge's body is covered with thousands of pores that allow water to flow through.

Different species, or kinds, of sponges live in different parts of the world. We know of about 5,000 different species of sponges. Scientists think there are about 5,000 more yet to be discovered. Most live in oceans, including the cold water near the North and South Poles. More than 150 kinds of freshwater sponges live in rivers, lakes, and streams.

Sponges live in nearly every kind of water on Earth.

pores

Simple Sponges

Sponges come in many different shapes and sizes. Some are tiny, while others are several feet tall. Some are brightly colored. No matter what they look like, all sponges are very simple. Sponges don't have a brain or **nervous system**. They don't have a heart, and they can't move around.

FOSSIL FACTS

Sponges attach themselves to solid surfaces in water where they can get enough food to live and grow.

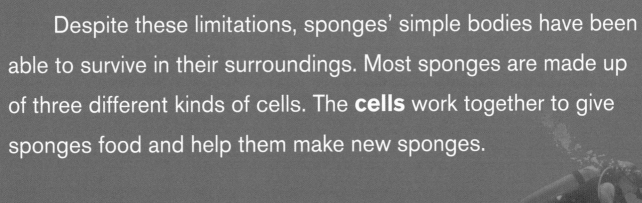

Despite these limitations, sponges' simple bodies have been able to survive in their surroundings. Most sponges are made up of three different kinds of cells. The **cells** work together to give sponges food and help them make new sponges.

Barrel sponges like the one shown here are big enough for a person to fit inside!

Cells Working Together

Sponges' simple bodies haven't changed much in all the time they've been on Earth. A sponge's body is hollow, but it has three **layers**. The outer layer is covered in pores. The middle, jellylike layer gives the sponge its shape. The inside layer is where the feeding begins!

Collar cells line the inside of a sponge. They're very sticky and capture tiny bits of food in the water that flows through the pores. Collar cells have a hairlike **flagellum** sticking out of them. The flagella move water through a sponge's pores.

FOSSIL FACTS

One kind of cell takes the sponge's food to other cells in its body.

pores

water flow

collar cell

flagellum

Water flows through the pores and out of the sponge through a big hole at the top.

Time to Eat

Sponges **filter** out food from the water that passes through them. Most of what sponges eat is too small for us to see. They eat tiny **bacteria** and a tiny type of animal called plankton.

Sponges are carnivores, which means they eat other animals. Scientists have found sponges that trap small animals with hooks on their treelike arms. They don't have mouths or teeth to chew, so these sponges use special liquids, called **enzymes**, to break down the animals' bodies.

FOSSIL FACTS

Some deep-sea sponges use collar cells to stir up water and create a current. The current draws their prey in, where it becomes dinner!

Many warm-water sponges live near coral **reefs**, which are home to many kinds of sea creatures. Reefs are a great place to find food!

Circle of Life

How do sponges make new sponges? They stay in one place, so they can't move to find a **mate**. Instead, some sponges send tiny male cells through the water to other sponges. Those cells come together with female cells to make new sponges. The baby sponges, called larvae, drift in the water until they find a solid place to stick and grow.

A small piece of a sponge can also break off, stick to something else, and start growing a new sponge. Sponges' ability to make new sponges in different ways has helped them survive over hundreds of millions of years.

This sponge is spawning, which is when sea animals let cells into the water in order to make new animals.

15

Helpers in the Ocean

Sponges are an important part of water **ecosystems**. Sponges that live on coral reefs take in bacteria that makes a gas called nitrogen. Too much or too little nitrogen can hurt the other plants and animals in the ecosystem. Sponges help keep the balance. Sponges can also help keep the population of certain plants and animals under control.

Sponges have few predators since their bodies don't have many **nutrients**. Scientists have found that some sponges can actually kill fish if the fish eat them. However, turtles, sea slugs, and sea stars eat some kinds of sponges.

This starfish is feeding on a sponge.

17

Sponge Divers

Humans have been using natural sponges to clean for thousands of years, even as far back as the ancient Greeks and Romans! Some ancient writings mention sponges, and long ago people made lots of money by bringing them out of the water.

These men lay sponges out to dry in the sun. Dried sponges can be used in many ways.

This practice still continues today. People dive deep into the waters of the Mediterranean Sea and off the coast of Florida searching for sponges. They cut them out of the water, bring them to land, and let them dry. Dried sponges can be used for cleaning and medicine, and some can even help cure illnesses.

dried sponges

Sponges in Trouble

Though sponges help us, the way we use them has sometimes hurt sponge populations. Taking too many from the water can upset the balance in their ecosystems. Sponges can also be hurt by fishing equipment that scrapes the ocean floor. Stopping this kind of fishing can help sponges on reefs stay safe.

Sponges are also affected by changes on our planet. As waters grow warmer and the weather changes, sponges must find ways to **adapt**.

FOSSIL FACTS

Glass sponges are growing very quickly in Antarctic waters. Scientists are trying to figure out why and how it will affect the ecosystems there.

This boat carries nets full of sponges. If too many sponges are taken from the water, the ecosystem will suffer.

More to Learn

Sponges have been a part of Earth's ocean ecosystems for ages, but there's still a lot to learn about them. New kinds of sponges are constantly being found, especially in deeper waters that are hard to reach.

It's our job to make sure we keep sponges and their ecosystems safe. These filtering friends can't move away from you, so if you see sponges living in reefs, make sure to leave them alone. These living fossils have a big job to do!

Glossary

adapt: To change to fit conditions.

bacteria: Tiny creatures that can only be seen with a microscope.

cell: The smallest basic part of a living thing.

ecosystem: A community of living things and the surroundings in which they live.

enzyme: A chemical produced by an animal that causes chemical reactions, or changes, to happen.

filter: To separate solid parts out of a liquid.

flagellum: A hairlike structure whose movements help pass water through a sponge's pores.

layer: One thickness laying over or under another.

mate: A partner for making babies.

nervous system: The network of cells that carries messages from the brain to other parts of the body.

nutrient: Something plants and animals need to survive.

oxygen: A gas people and other animals need to breathe in order to live.

reef: A ridge of rocks or coral near the surface of the water.

Index

Websites

Due to the changing nature of Internet links, PowerKids Press has developed an online list of websites related to the subject of this book. This site is updated regularly. Please use this link to access the list: www.powerkidslinks.com/fos/spon

DATE DUE

			PRINTED IN U.S.A.